GUN

Ancient Gunn

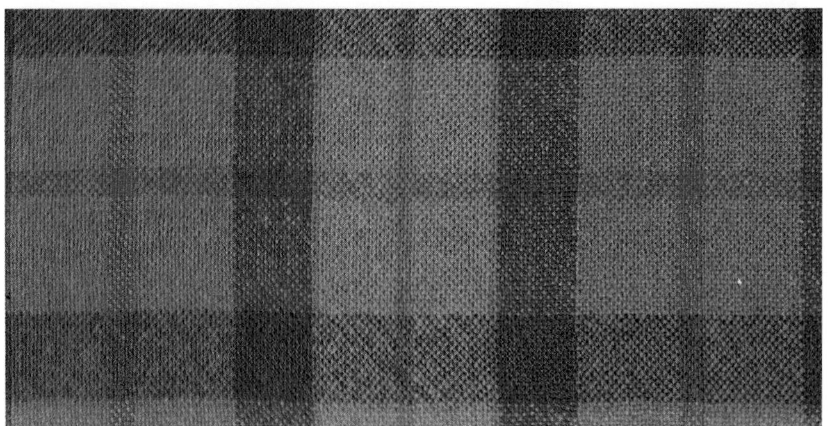

Weathered Gunn

Modern Gunn

CLAN GUNN

Extensively Revised

COMPILED BY
Alan McNie

CASCADE PUBLISHING COMPANY
Jedburgh, Scotland

Genealogical Research:
Research regrettably cannot be undertaken by the publisher. A non-profit organisation, The Scots Ancestry Research Society, 3 Albany Street, Edinburgh, undcrtake research for an agreed fee.

Rowandene, Belses, Jedburgh, Scotland

ISBN 0 90761485 X

Page 1 Explanation:
The illustrated tartan is the Ancient Gunn. The motto on the clan badge means, 'Either peace or war'. In the artist's montage the Clan Gunn Heritage Centre, which is located in the Old Parish Church at Latheron in Caithness, is depicted. Also illustrated in the foreground is Juniper, a clan plant badge.

Gunn Country

The map used below and on the following page is intended basically as a pictorial reference. It is accurate enough, however, to be correlated with a current map. The clan boundaries are only marginally correct. No precise boundaries were kept in early times and territories were fluctuating frequently.

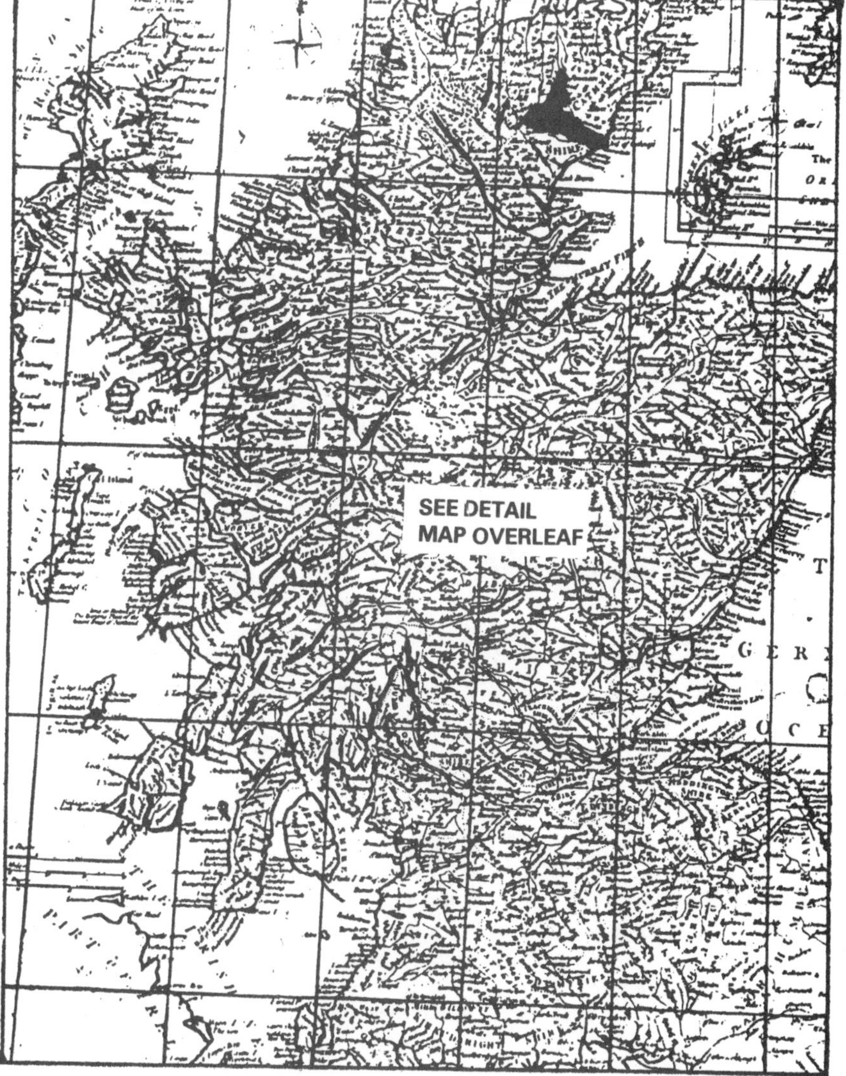

Gunn

CLAN MAP

1. **Berriedale Castle** Ruins close to clan country

2. **Braemore** One of branches formed after death of George Gunn of Ulbster

3. **Castles Sinclair and Girnigoe** Much clan rivalry with Sinclair centred here

4. **Dirlot Castle** Gunns involved in battle

5. **Dunrobin Castle** Strong Clan Gunn influence for centuries

6. **Harberry Castle** Clyth early clan seat

7. **Harpsdale** Bloody battle between Keiths and Gunns in 1426

8. **Helmsdale** Important coastal village for clan

9. **Killernan** Clan seat after Harberry Castle

10. **Latheron** Clan Gunn Museum in parish church

11. **Navidale** Gunns settled here for long time

12. **Ulbster** Strong clan association

Wick
Dunbeath Castle
Langwell
Berrydale Castle
Ord of Caithness
Lothmore
Clyn Irish
Dunrobin
Golospie
Tarbat Ness
Tarbat Castle
Dornock
Taine
Cathow C
Sandwick
Coutinade
Firth of Cromarty
Cromarty
Knockennen Castle

Castles Sinclair and Girnigoe *Closely involved in clan rivalry*

CLAN GUNN

Condensed from Clans of the Highlands of Scotland,
Thomas Smibert, 1850

Most writers on the annals of the Scottish Highlanders do not reckon the Clan Gunn as among the septs entitled to a full or separate notice at all. It strikes us, however, that they are perhaps among the very purest remmants of the Gael to be found about Sutherlandshire and the adjoining parts. So thinks Stewart of Garth, obviously, since he takes care in mapping the territories of the clans, to allude to Sutherlandshire as including the Gunns or Clan Guinn. It is probable that they belong mainly to the same stock which produced the great body of the Sutherland population, that later name having been adopted, as already explained, from the title given to the region by the Norsemen, and not being connected with the true origin of the Gaelic natives.

There are several stories on record respecting the descent of the Gunns (Guns or Guins). The same old family genealogist, who was cited respecting the race of Gilleandris (a name changed successively into Gilleanrias, Leandris, Anrias, Rias, and lastly Ross), calls the first Guin one of "three brethern, Guin, Leod, and Leandris, who come out of Denmark, to the north pairts of Scotland, to follow their fortune; and Guin took possession of the Braes of Cathnes, where

Helmsdale *A coastal village in clan country*

his posterity remanes to this day, called the Clan Gunn." The continuation of the tale is that Leod founded the Macleod sept; and we admitted it to be probably true that the Macleods of the Isles really had a liberal share of Norse blood in their veins, though the account here mentioned had little weight in causing that decision. As distinctly was it stated, however, that the Clan Ross appeared to us to be almost purely of the native Gaelic race. Of the Clan Gunn the same opinion must be expressed. The name seems to be Gaelic or Celtic, and identical with that of Gwynne, so common among the Celts or Gwaelsh of the west of England. The word in the Erse tongue has certain meanings, rendering it not inappropriate as a name for a wild tribe of mountaineers in the old-days. As a substantive, *guin* signifies "fierceness", and also "pain", "a wound", "a sting", "a dart"; while, as a verb, it means "to wound, pierce, or sting"; and, as an adjective, framed from the same root, it has the sense of "sharp, keen, bitterly malicious". So say Drs Norman Macleod and Daniel Dewar in their Gaelic dictionary. It therefore seems likely that *guin* was a generic term applied to some of the rudest and most northerly of the Scottish Highlanders in very early times, as well as to the hillmen of Wales, similarly situated. The name of the *Siol Cuinn,* applied to the Highlanders of Argyle, is probably the very same name. However, the names are now Gunn and Wynne, according to the common modes of spelling. Even the definite arrangement of families into all the varieties of Macs, which formed a sort of approach on the part of the more inland Highlanders to the usages of civilised life, appears to have been unknown in the far north. This supposition is strengthened by the fact, that the Gael on the most southerly borders of the Highlands surpassed the inland tribes in regularity of nomenclature, as much as these did the ultra-northerns. The names of Farquharson, Robertson and Ferguson, within the Perth and Forfar limits, exemplify what is here meant.

In short, we repeat our belief that the name of Gunn had a generic origin, indicating a "fierce" tribe; and that they had been so christened by those around them who first possessed or attained to any knowledge of the art of nomenclature, or had occasion for its use. Nor need the Clan Gunn distress themselves about the barbarism thus "nominally" imputed to their sires. Even the general name of "Scots" appears to come from an Erse term signifying, in its mildest sense, "wanderers"; the Belgae, again, were "ravagers"; while multitudes of other entire nations cannot boast even of such decent sources for their designations. These, however, became commonly permanent, simply because the Romans (in most instances) moulded the primitive terms which struck their fancy, or came in their way, into their own tongue, in referring to the countries conquered by them; and because nearly all the early learning of these said countries sprung from and through them, the first native historians having no other *written* languages at command, save the classical ones, and especially the Latin. It may be thought that this subject has been too much dwelt upon, considering the Gunns to have long been but a secondary sept of Sutherlandshire; but, in reality, the question has a general bearing. Such native stories as that of "Guin the Dane" cannot stand, in our eyes, against the more common-sense view of the subject, although these stories may be found in manuscripts two or three hundred years old. One word of one able and educated historian is generally of far greater worth than hundreds of merely traditional tales recorded by men unknown, and men for the most part plainly unqualified for the task of repeating even hearsays of hearsays correctly and intelligibly. Every person of ordinary sense must have noticed, besides, how inconsistent is the conduct commonly of those who love to refer to old MSS. They will often laugh loudly when pointing to witch-stories, appearances of the devil, and so forth; and yet in the next sentence will they gravely accept the reports of these authorities on ancient genealogical and historical questions of moment, though the same blinded ignorance must have actuated the writers on the one point as well as the others, and though sound and really credible annalists may have told a very different tale.

Ed. Note: Today it is known this clan is of Norse origin

The Gunns are represented as living mainly, as far as they were a separate sept, to the north of Dunrobin Castle, which stands on the eastern coast of Sutherlandshire. They had chieftains of their own name, though these might hold a second place in respect of the Sutherland earls; and they had a castle of their own, called Halbury. Several traditions respecting the Gunns are current in their native district. The following is curious, if it were but from the names. The "Keiths" mentioned are plainly the men of *Kaith*ness merely; and the word "crowner" (if we are to interpret the Gaelic word *chruner* as

Old Dunrobin Castle

crowner) seems to imply merely the judicial agent or representative of the superior lords of the country.

Towards the end of the fifteenth century, the chief of the Clan Gun (or Gunn, here adopted as the best form of the name) was George Gunn, who lived in feudal dignity in his then impregnable castle of Halbury; but he was better known as *Crowner Gunn*, or, as he was called by the Highlanders, *"N'm Braistach-more,"* from a great brooch which he wore as the badge or cognisance of his office of crowner. He had a deadly feud with the chief of the Keiths; and having met in St Tyre's chapel for the purpose of effecting a reconciliation, but without success, they were solemnly agreed to decide their quarrel, if they could not do so amicably on a future day, by equal combat between twelve sons or relatives of each chieftain. The crowner and the leader of the Keiths approached each other in full armour; but it was soon discovered by the Gunns that there were two riders on every horse in the party of the Keiths, and consequently the latter party had twenty-four men opposed to the twelve followers of the crowner. This vile stratagem instantly revealed to the Gunns that their destruction, by unfair means, was determined upon. They scorned, notwithstanding the great odds against them, to retreat before their enemies, the Keiths; and fought most desperately, but could not withstand the great odds that opposed them. After a long-continued struggle, the survivors on both sides were so much exhausted, that the combat was mutually dropped – the Keiths being so far the victors as to leave the field with their banner displayed, and to be able to carry with them their slain companions; while in the ranks of the Gunns, the crowner and seven of his party were killed, and the remaining five were all severely wounded. The Keiths proceeded to Dilred Castle, in Strathmore, then occupied by Sutherland of Dilred, where they were hospitably entertained. The five surviving Gunns, who were all sons of the crowner, also retired, but tarried at another stream, since then called Alt-Torquil, after Torquil Gunn, one of the survivors, who there dressed the wounds of his brothers. Towards evening, Henry-beg, the youngest of the surviving brothers of the Gunns, proposed that they should follow the Keiths, and endeavour to obtain revenge, even by stratagem such as the Keiths had recourse to. They arrived at Dilred Castle soon after nightfall. On approaching the castle, its wooden windows or shutters were found open, and around a large fire in the lowest apartment the survivors of the Keiths were quaffing bumpers of ale; and Henry, who went close to one of the windows, heard them narrate, with boisterous delight, the losses sustained by the Gunns. The chief of the Keiths, not apprehensive of any danger, accidentally approached the window where Henry stood, and the latter then bent his bow, and in another instant his arrow pierced the chieftain's heart; Henry at the same time boldly accompanying the deadly flight of his arrow with the exclamation (afterwards used in the North Highlands as a proverb) of "The Gunn's compliments to Keith". The old

Earl of Moray *Had Gunn chief executed for not giving way in street*

Edinburgh Castle *Gunn chief imprisoned for illegally burning corn stalks*

chief dropped down dead; a panic seized the other Keiths; and the three Gunns, having darted forward to the door of the castle, slew some of the first persons who ventured out by it; but finding that they could not retain their position long, Henry and his two brothers retired silently under cover of the darkness of the night, and hurried back to the assistance of the other brothers, who had been unable to accompany them."

Other stories are told of the Gunns, but their history in old days, as observed, is chiefly mixed up with the general annals of the Sutherland and Caithness tribes. In the "Genealogical History of the Earldom of Sutherland," written up to 1630 by Sir Robert Gordon of Gordonstone, and continued to 1651 by another party, several notices of the Clan Gunn occur incidentally. At a skirmish which took place A.D. 1517 "William Mackames-Wick-*Chrune* (the name being plainly the same as "Crowner" just noticed), cheeff of the Clan Gunn in Southerland", was present against the Mackys or Mackays, and gave them a signal defeat, two or three hundred men being slain on the unsuccessful side. The exact words of Sir R. Gordon, writing not very long afterwards, are – "Their wer two hundred of the Strathnaver men slian, theirtie-two of the Seill (Siol) Faill, and fyfteen of the Seill-Thomas." The commander of the vanquished in this affair is called "Neill-Mackean-Mack-Angus;" and his brother is styled John Moir-Mackean, from whom "descended a race of people called the Slaight-Ean-Voir", which means the race of John the Great. The whole of this extract proves accuracy in Gaelic nomenclature to be a point utterly unattainable. Indeed, this battle with the "Mackys" may only be a version of the fight with the Keiths. The name of Keith (odd as it may seem) is easily changed into Mac-Kays, or Mac-Kaiths. The common source of the people is further made obvious, in reality.

Sir Robert Gordon proceeds to say, that "William Mackames (cheiftane of the Clangun), heer mentioned, was called Cattigh. He wes borne and bred in Southerland. From him are descended the Clangun that dwell at this day in Strathully. They hae alwyse since that tyme had the lands of Killeirnan for ther service, from the Earles of Southerland, unto whom they have ever been both trusty and faithfull."

It is plain, from these and other incidents, that the people of Sutherland, Caithness, and Moray, were always named from their localities when viewed *en masse,* and from their immediate sires when

Clan Gunn Museum

spoken of specially, having no baptismal registrations. The Sutherland men are spoken of always as fighting with southern parties of the name of "John-Roy-Moray", and such like; or else they fought with Mackians or Mackys, on their northern borders. Mackames (which means Macjames or Machamish) seems to be the oldest Gaelic sept-name of the Gunns. The point is not of peculiar moment, the conclusion being clear that they are true Celtic Highlanders.

At the close of the sixteenth century, there seem indeed to have occurred bloody feuds betwixt the Sutherland and Caithness men, or, in other words, betwixt the Gunns and a branch of the Mackays. Sir Robert Gordon says, that the horrible encounters, the bloodshed, the spoiling, together with "their asperous names", prevent him from giving details. The Clan Gunn appear to have come by the worst at times between the Caithness and Sutherland earls. At a meeting of the two (says Sir Robert Gordon) "it wes concluded amongst them that some of the Clangun should be *made away*;" and the poor Clan Gunn seemed destined to destruction. The business ended in that final separation of the Gunns from the Mackays and Sinclairs, to whom they had been before attached, which has been mentioned. Sir R. Gordon says, on the subject of the tribe: – "The Clangun are a race of people dwelling within the diocese of Catteness, and are divyded among the thrie countries of Southerland, Catteness and Strathnaver. They are verie couragious, rather desperat then valiant." They came at last from under the power of the Mackays and Sinclairs, as said, and such of the tribe as have still dwelt in Southerland have ever been faithful to their masters, the earls of Southerland. Their "commander and chieftane is called Mack-wick-Kames, and remaineth alwyse in Killiernan in Strathully, wher he hath some landes and possessions from the earles of Southerland, as a fee for his service." Alluding to his own time, the chronicler adds and interpolates the remark, that "John Robson (Mackames), chiftain of the Clangun in Catteness, did now of late, the yeir of God 1618, mak his refuge of Southerland, having fallen out with the Earle of Catteness and Macky; so that this whole surname doth for the present depend altogether upon the house of Southerland."

It was in the year 1586 that the Gunns were pursued both by the men of Caithness and Sutherland. Almost by chance they fought the

Dunnottar Castle *Former clan seat of Keiths*

former, and beat them. This proved the critical event in the fortunes of the Gunn family. At first, indeed, both the Caithness and Sutherland earls turned their powers against the sept, and took captive the next chief, George (Mack-ean Mack-rob) Gunn, after a skirmish in which he fought most stoutly, and, being vanquished, threw himself into a lake, "sore-wounded", to make a last struggle for life and liberty. After being liberated, as it is said, he attached himself to the party to whom he deemed himself most deeply indebted, the Earl of Sutherland; and the clan and family became fixed adherents, as related, of that noble house. It was not until the year 1619, however, that they were formally dispossessed of all their lands held under the Caithness family, and also of their holdings under the Mackays; whereupon the whole "retired themselves, with their families, into Sutherland". Alexander (Davidson or) Gunn and his race were placed by Sir Robert Gordon in Strathully. Some small portions of the old Caithness possessions, however, were afterwards recovered.

It is clear, from this whole and rather confused story, that the Gunns had been a branch of the purest aborigines of the north. The Sinclairs and such like baronial incomers might gain the upper hand as rulers through regal favours and other causes; but they could not materially change the breed of the people.

The Chiefship of Clan Gunn has lain dormant for over a 100 years so in 1972 the amigerous and landed members of the Clan applied to the Lord Lyon King of Arms to appoint a Head of the Clan until such time as the Chief can be traced, and he appointed Iain Gunn of Banniskirk to be Commander (Ceanna Cath) of the Clan.

On the 28th July, 1978 Commander Iain Gunn of Banniskirk, together with Lord Kintore, Chief of the Keiths, signed a treaty at Ackergill which ended the 500 year old feud between the Gunns and the Keiths.

On the Gunn side this had been organized by the Clan Gunn Society, originally founded in Thurso in 1821 and revived by Iain Gunn of Banniskirk in Edinburgh in 1960.

Caves of Smoo *Scenic wonder a few miles from Clan Gunn country*

Gunn Associated Names

Associated names have a hazy history. Sometimes they had more than one origin; also clouding the precise location of a particular surname might be that name's proscription or of course a migrant population. Even the spelling of surnames was subject to great variations, shifting from usually Latin or Gaelic and heeding rarely to consistent spelling. In early records there can be several spellings of the same name. Undoubtedly contributing to this inconsistency is the handwriting in official records, which was often open to more than one spelling interpretation.

With regard to the 'Mac' prefix, this was, of course, from the Gaelic meaning, son of. It wasn't long before it was abbreviated to 'Mc' or 'M', until we have reached the position now where there are more 'Mc's' than 'Mac's'.

GALLIE, GALLY From the Gaelic 'gallaich', foreigners and therefore of Norse origin. The Gunns of Caithness were expelled after 1589 and the ones that settled in Rossshire near Tain became known as Gallie, i.e. foreigners. Patrick Gallie owned a tenement in Irvine in 1426. The name is on decline now.

GANSON, GAUNSON, GAWENSON Son of Gavin or Gaven. Gaunson may also be a form of 'Gunn's son', The name is common in Caithness, the original seat of Clan Gunn. Alexander Gawenstone lived in Nairn in 1563.

GAULDIE, GALDIE A form of Gallie and therefore connected to the Gunns. James Gauldie of Pitchaish was a prisoner in the Jacobite rebellion of '45.

GEORGESON Son of George. Robert Georgeson was the son of George Gunn, Crowner of Caithness, died 1464, from whom the majority of the septs of clan Gunn are descended. William Georgeson was a tenant in Coupar Grange in 1471.

HENDERSON Son of Henry. Henry was the 4th son of George Gunn, Crowner of Caithness and the families of this branch are descended from him. When George Gunn and several of his brothers were killed by the Keiths, Henry separated from the rest of the family and settled in Caithness. William Henrison, Snr., was, in 1374, chamberlain of Lochmaben Castle (9 ml NE Dumfries). James Hendirsoune was witness in Glasgow in 1553.

JAMESON, JAMIESON Son of James. James was another son of George Gunn, Crowner, and became chief after his death. William Jamyson lived in Pollock in 1472 (Glasgow). John Jamezing was given a reprieve for his part in the murder of John, Earl of Caithness in 1539.

JOHNSON Son of John. The Johnsons of Caithness are descended from John, 3rd son of George Gunn, Crowner of Caithness. Both were killed by the Keiths. Wautier Jonessone gave homage in 1296 in Berwickshire. Adam Jonesson was a prisoner of war in Newgate prison in 1375 and Malcolm Jonis was an important man in Orkney in 1427.

KEAN, KEAND, KEENE, KWEN From MacKean which is a form of MacIan meaning son of John. From the same ancestry as Johnson. James Kewne lived in Borgue (6 ml SW of Kirkcudbright) in 1684.

MAGNUS From the Latin, meaning Great. An old Norse personal name. St Magnus was uncle of St Ronald of Orkney, a forefather of Ragnhild, wife of Gunni from whom the name Gunn was derived. The Gunn family burial place was St Magnus' Chapel at Spital (5 ml from Dirlot Castle). Magnus Caddenheid lived in Cortance in Aberdeen in 1633.

MANSON Form of Magnusson, son of Magnus. This name is very common in Shetland and Caithness and is of ancient origin. There was a Norse chieftain named Magnus mac Arailt in the Hebrides in 972. Manson was both Mary Queen of Scots and James VI's carpenter. The name is a sept of Clan Gunn.

MAIN, MAUN, MANUS Form of Magnus. John Mane was a tenant in Kelso in 1567. Andro Man was executed in Aberdeen for witchcraft in 1597.

MACMANUS From Gaelic 'MacMaghnuis' son of Magnus. John M'Manis was a witness in Dunbretane in 1506.

MACKEAN, MACKEAND, MCKAIN, MCKEN Forms of MacIan, son of John. Related to Gunns through John son of George Gunn. (See Johnson). In 1651 Andrew MaKaynd was confined to the pillory for abusing the magistrates in Elgin. Nigel McCane lived in Islay in 1506.

MACROB, MACROBB Son of Robb. Descended from Robert son of George Gunn, Crowner of Caithness. In 1458 Henry McRob was Mayor of Menteith. Andrew M'Robe was witness in Loch Leven in 1546.

MACWILLIAM, MACQUILLIAM, MACKILLIAM From the Gaelic 'Mac Uilleim', son of William. Descendants of William, 5th son of George Gunn, Crowner of Caithness. There was a Gillecrist Makwilliam living in the Black Isle in 1500. Henry Makwilliam was vicar of Logie-Mar in 1521. (4 ml W Tarland).

NEILSON, NIELSON, NILSON, NELSON Son of Neil. There were two divisions of this name, the Neilsons of Caithness and of Craigcaffie. It is no doubt the Neilsons of Caithness are the sect connected to the Gunns, Caithness being the seat of the Gunns.

ROBINSON Son of Robert, son of George Gunn, Crowner of Caithness. Robin was a diminutive of Robert as early as 1483. John Robynson had a tenement in Irvine in 1426. This name was common in Glasgow in the 16th century.

ROBSON Son of Rob or Robert. The Robsons in the North are descended from George Gunn, Crowner of Caithness or from John Gunn Robson who lived around 1616. John Robison was a vicar near Kelso in 1475. Andrew Robson was named heir of Glediswode, Lauderdale.

SANDISON, SANDESON Sandy's son, diminutive of Alexander. Probably descended from George Gunn by Chief Alexander Machamish Gunn or Alexander Georgeson. There was a Thomas Sandson living in Shetland in 1491.

SWANN, SWAN, SWAIN Not known before 1033. This sept of the Gunn clan is said to be descended from Sweyn who was a pirate and brother of the first Gunn, who settled in Caithness. Swan Thore was a witness at Madderty in 1189. Thorus filuis Swani was a witness in Perth in 1130.

SWANSON, SWAINSON Son of Swan. A name found mostly in Caithness, seat of the Gunns. Alanus filius Swani was a witness in Tubermor in 1298. (Tobermory Bay, 28 ml WNW of Oban).

WILLIAMSON Son of William. The Williamsons are a sept of the Gunns being the descendants of a later chief of the Gunns. Adam son of William was associated with the accounts of Peebles in 1343. There were Williamsons in Banniskirk, Caithness in 1665. David Williamson, minister of St Cuthberts in Edinburgh; Dainty Davie in song; outlived 6 wives and the 7th outlived him.

WILLS, WILSON, WILLSON, WILSONE All these names signify son of Will and in the north refer to William, George Gunn's son. It was a well known name in Glasgow in the 16th century. Michael Wilsoun was burgess of Aberdeen in 1418. David Visone and Pait Vilsoun were tenants of Kelso in 1567.

WYLIE, WYLLIE A form of William. William Wyly was a witness in Prestwick in Ayrshire in 1446. John Weyle paid rent in Carstairs in 1530.

Name of Individual or Head of Family.	Occupation.	Place of Residence.	Age of Head.	No. of Children. Above 12.	Under 12.	Meal supplied per lbs.	Other Supplies.	Remarks.	By subscribing in this Column, the Parties receiving the Supply agree to work or pay therefor.	
James Gunn	Do & Fisher	Burrigh	44		6	42		+ Wife in Destitution	Do	4
Archd. Sutherland	Do & Cooper	Ashbeg	53	2	2	28		+ Do Do Idle during the winter	Do	5
James Gunn	Hill of Forn	Crofter	41	1	4	28		+ Wife Destitute	Do	6
Hugh Mackay	Crofter & Fisher	Roadside	38		8	42		+ Do Do	Do	7
Hector Sutherland	Do Do	Forn	40		6	42		+ Do very Do	Do	8
John Nicoll	Do Do	Rhimigie	52	3	3	42		+ Do " Do	Do	9
Widow Geo. Sutherland	Crofter	Burrigh	60			14		Do	Do	10
Henry Gunn	Do	Hill of Forn	40			14		Do	Do	11
Willm. Sinclair	Do & Fisher	Do	34		2	28		Do	Do	12
Alex. Mackay	Crofter	Lochend	76			28		+ Wife Do	Do	13
Wm Cormack	Do	Hill of Forn	72			28		+ Do Do	Do	14
Peter Sutherland	Do	Rumster	65	2	2	28		+ Do Do	Do	15
Cath. Nicoll	Subtenant	Crofter	28		3	21		Husband South for work family Destitute	Do	16
Sinclair Sutherland	Crofter	Hill of Forn	60	2	2	28		+ Wife Destitute	Do	17
Kirstian Nicoll	Do	Do	53			14		Do	Do	18
Robert Macdonald	Do	Rumster	34		4	28		+ Wife Do	Do	19
Alex. Mackenzie	Do	Do	53	3		28		+ Do Do	Do	20
Jas. Munro	Do	Binchelt	40		4	28		+ Do Do	Do	21

courtesy Scottish Records Office

1847 Register of Destitute from Ulbster. Many of the listed, including three Gunns, would

Berriedale Castle *Adjacent to coastal clan territory*

Clan Background Excerpts from Book Referred to on Facing Page

The coat armour is arg., a galley of three masts, sails furled and oars in action, sab., displaying at the mast-head, flags, gu., within a bordure, az. On a chief of the third, a bear's head of the first, muzzled of the second, between two mullets of the field. Crest, a dexter arm wielding a broadsword, proper. Motto, "Aut pax aut bellum."

The suicheanas, or badge, is Craobh Aitean, *juniperis communis,* juniper bush.

The most ancient seat of the chief was Hallburg, a fortress then deemed impregnable; latterly they inhabited the castle of Kilearnan, which was unfortunately destroyed by fire in the year 1690.

The Gunn tartan will be seen from the figure to be of a fine dark pattern which, like that worn by the clansmen of Roderic dubh, served so well to conceal an ambuscade among the sombre-coloured and luxurant heath and mountain herbage. The coat is madar, a colour produced by a native vegetable dye.

The McIan illustration of Gunn as published (mid-19th century) in 'The Clans of the Scottish Highlands'

Excerpts from

PARISH LIFE IN THE NORTH OF SCOTLAND

BY THE

LATE REV. DONALD SAGE, A.M.

MINISTER OF RESOLIS

WICK, 1899

Extracts concern 'Gunns' he encountered

Page 39: This section written by the author's son

I have often heard my father speak of those with whom he was on terms of intimacy during his ministry at Dirlot. MARCUS GUNN, his next neighbour, was a man of decided piety. He lived at Dalmore, in the immediate neighbourhood, while his brother lived at Cattaich, also in the vicinity, and each had a large family of sons. Marcus Gunn was lessee of the original estate of Dirlot, comprising Dirlot, Dalmore, Dalnaclaitan. Toremisdale, and Cattaich, and these pendicles of his farm he had sub-let to his own near relatives, presiding over them with all the simplicity and affection of a patriarch. His lease he held of the laird of Ulbster, who, in the year that my father came to Dirlot, was created a Baronet as Sir John Sinclair. Patrick, one of Marcus Gunn's sons, presented my father with a fine folio copy of Bishop Pearson's Exposition of the Creed, now in my possession.

Page 132:

Close by John Meadhonach's house at Kildonan stood that of DONALD GUNN, one of the tightest and most active of Highlanders. Indeed, every possible element which entered into the structure of this man's mind, as well as into the size and make of his body, combined to constitute him the very model of a Highland peasant. He was exactly of the middle size, and well made, with just as much flesh on his bones as simply served to cover them, and no more. He had a face full of expression, which conveyed most unequivocally the shrewdness, cunning, acuteness and caustic humour so strongly characteristic of his race. Donald Gunn surpassed his whole neighbourhood and, perhaps, the whole parish, in all rustic and athletic exercises. At a brawl, in which, however, he but seldom engaged, none could exceed him in the dexterity and rapidity with which he brandished his cudgel; and though many might exceed him in physical strength, his address and alert activity often proved him more than a match for an assailant of much greater weight and size. Then in dancing he was without a rival. With inimitable ease and natural grace he kept time, with eye and foot and fingers, to all the minute modulations of a Highland reel or Strathspey. He was also a good shot, a successful deer stalker, angler, smuggler, and poacher. Donald, however, with all these secular and peculiarly Highland recommendations, was little better than a heathen. He was always under suspicion, and latterly made some hair-breadth escapes from the gallows, for he was, by habit and repute, a most notorious thief. His wife, Esther Sutherland, was a native of Caithness, and a very handsome woman. His daughter Janet married a man Bruce from Loist, and Jane married a Malcolm Fraser, who was afterwards drowned at Helmisdale. His son Robert went to America with Lord Selkirk's colony, and in an affray between these settlers and those of the North-West Company poor Robert Gunn was killed.

Page 137:

ROBERT GUNN of Achaneccan was another of the old men of my youthful remembrance. He was the acknowledged lineal descendant and representative of the chiefs of Clan Gunn in the parish; although that landless and fallen honour was some years afterwards claimed by Hector Gunn of Thurso, whose only son became factor to the Duke of Sutherland. Robert of Achaneccan was, however, unquestionably nearer of kin. His farm, on which he had a number of sub-tenants, was scarcely two miles distant from Kinbrace, the seat of his renowned ancestor. He was a gentleman-like old man, who had been much in good society, and had received a somewhat liberal education. His descendants are still to be found here and there in the county of Caithness.

Page 210:

One Lieutenant Gunn lived at Ach-na-h'uaighe. He held the place in lease from the proprietor for nineteen years, which commenced four or five years before I came to Achness. He married a Miss Bruce of Thurso, a woman of colour, daughter of Mr Harry Bruce, a West Indian planter, by whom he got some money, which was soon dissipated. They had a large family. After the dispersion of the tenantry in 1819, Gunn, for a compensation, resigned his lease and went to reside, first at Thurso, and afterwards at Balfruch, parish of Croy, which he held from Davidson of Cantray. He died at Inverness in 1844.

Page 307:

The next day we went to Watten, where, on the 29th September, I preached. Mr Fraser left us, intending to preach at Wick on Sabbath, October 2nd, and I remained with Mr Gunn until the Saturday. During my residence in Caithness I had become slightly acquainted with him, but this was the first time that I had the opportunity fully to enter into and to estimate the excellency of his Christian and ministerial character. The simplicity of his faith, the soundness of his views, and the heaven-tending earnestness of his spirit made me feel that, while I was scarce a disciple, he was truly a master in Israel.* The intimates of his home at the time were his excellent helpmate, the daughter of Mr Arthur, my immediate predecessor at Resolis, and a sweet-looking girl of about seventeen, his brother's daughter.

*Mr Alexander Gunn, A.M., a native of Caithness, was ordained at Orphir, Orkney, in 1803, and admitted minister of Watten 26th September, 1805. He was a preacher of eminent ability and evangelical power. His church became a centre of attraction for the people of Caithness, and his ministry was fruitful in spiritual blessing to many. He died 28th August, 1836, in the 63rd year of his age and 33rd of his ministry. His son Alexander (who has completed the 50th year of this ministry) succeeded him on the 6th April, 1837. – Ed.

Some Clan Notables

Frederick Gunn, a native of Washington, Connecticut, was born in 1816. Both an educator and innovator he opened and taught at several schools. A principled man, he was forced to leave one school because of his strong abolitional views. His greatest length of teaching time was spent at a family school in Washington he called The Gunnery.

Donald Gunn was born in Halkirk, Caithness in 1797. He entered the service of the Hudson's Bay Company in 1813. In 1871 he was appointed a member of the Legislative Council of Manitoba. He contributed a number of papers on the natural history of the North West to the Miscellaneous Collections of the Smithsonian Institute.

Ronald and William Gunn, two brothers who were sons of a Caithness native both contributed significantly to Australian life. Ronald (1808-1881) held several posts in penal administration and estate management. The latter encouraged a vital interest in botany. Following retirement he became deputy commissioner for Northern Tasmania. Few Tasmanian plants alluded this outstanding botanist. His botanical efforts are commemorated today by the genus Gunnia. Ronald Gunn's brother, William, also had a distinguished career. He commanded soldiers against bushrangers: in one encounter he lost his arm. He received a series of appointments in the penal service. In 1850 he also became a police magistrate.

ACKNOWLEDGEMENTS

We are indebted to staff members of the Hawick Library and Scottish Room, Edinburgh City Libraries for their generous assistance. Research work done by Barbara Blackburn has proved valuable and thorough.